Wheels, Wings, and Water

Shapes to Go

Lola M. Schaefer

Heinemann Library
Chicago, Illinois

Designed by Sue Emerson, Heinemann Library; Page layout by Que-Net Media
Printed and bound in the United States by Lake Book Manufacturing, Inc.
Photo research by Amor Montes De Oca

07 06 05 04 03
10 9 8 7 6 5 4 3 2 1

Library of Congress Cataloging-in-Publication Data
Schaefer, Lola M., 1950-
   Shapes to go / Lola M. Schaefer.
       v. cm. – (Wheels, wings, and water)
Includes index.
Contents: Shapes are everywhere – Shapes on aircraft – Shapes on bicycles – Shapes on boats – Shapes on cars – Shapes on fire trucks – Shapes on motorcycles – Shapes on spacecraft – Shapes on trains.
   ISBN 1-4034-0886-6 (HC), 1-4034-3622-3 (Pbk.)
   1. Motor vehicles–Juvenile literature. 2. Geometry–Juvenile literature. 3. Form perception–Juvenile literature.
[1. Motor vehicles. 2. Shape. 3. Form perception.] I. Title. II. Series.
   TL147.S37 2003
   629.04'6–dc21

2002014725

Acknowledgments
The author and publishers are grateful to the following for permission to reproduce copyright material:
p. 4 Kevin Fleming/Corbis; p. 5 Stone/Getty Images; p. 6 Stuart Westmorland/Corbis; p. 7 Richard Hamilton Smith/Corbis; pp. 8, 11 Corbis; p. 9 Philip Gould/Corbis; p. 10 Jeff Greenberg/Visuals Unlimited; p. 12 Science VU/Visuals Unlimited; p. 13 Ariel Skelley/Corbis; pp. 14, 15 Amor Montes de Oca; p. 16 H. Rogers/TRIP; p. 17 P. Treanor/TRIP; p. 18 Marc Epstein/Visuals Unlimited; p. 19 Science VU/NASA/Visuals Unlimited; p. 20 Colin Garrett/Milepost 92 1/2/Corbis; p. 21 Gary J. Benson; p. 22 row 1 (L-R) Science VU/Visuals Unlimited, Amor Montes De Oca; row 2 (L-R) Marc Epstein/Visuals Unlimited, Richard Hamilton Smith/Corbis; p. 23 row 1 (L-R) Richard Hamilton Smith/Corbis, P. Treanor/TRIP; row 2 (L-R) Colin Garrett/Milepost 92 1/2/Corbis, Corbis, Stuart Westmorland/Corbis, Gary J. Benson; row 3 Marc Epstein/Visuals Unlimited; row 4 (L-R) PhotoDisc, Philip Gould/Corbis, Science VU/NASA/Visuals Unlimited; p. 24 row 1 (L-R) Science VU/Visuals Unlimited, Amor Montes De Oca; row 2 (L-R) Marc Epstein/Visuals Unlimited, Richard Hamilton Smith/Corbis; back cover (L-R) Science VU/Visuals Unlimited, Corbis

Cover photographs by Erwin Nielsen/Visuals Unlimited, Mug Shots/Corbis, Patrik Giardino/Corbis

Every effort has been made to contact copyright holders of any material reproduced in this book. Any omissions will be rectified in subsequent printings if notice is given to the publisher.

Special thanks to our advisory panel for their help in the preparation of this book:

Alice Bethke, Library Consultant
Palo Alto, CA

Eileen Day, Preschool Teacher
Chicago, IL

Kathleen Gilbert,
Second Grade Teacher
Round Rock, TX

Sandra Gilbert,
Library Media Specialist
Fiest Elementary School
Houston, TX

Jan Gobeille,
Kindergarten Teacher
Garfield Elementary
Oakland, CA

Angela Leeper,
Educational Consultant
North Carolina Department
of Public Instruction
Wake Forest, NC

Some words are shown in bold, **like this.**
You can find them in the picture glossary on page 23.

Contents

Shapes Are Everywhere

There are shapes that stand still.

There are **circles**, **squares**, and **triangles**.

There are shapes that go, too.

There are **rectangles** and **ovals.**

Shapes on Aircraft

There are shapes on aircraft.

The wings on this **seaplane** are **rectangles**.

This **blimp** is a large balloon.

Its body looks like an **oval**.

Shapes on Bicycles

There are shapes on bicycles.

This bicycles **frame** makes
a **triangle**.

This bicycle **pedal** is shaped like a **rectangle**.

Bicycle wheels are shaped like **circles**.

Shapes on Boats

There are shapes on boats.

These sailboats have sails that are large **triangles**.

paddle

A **kayak** paddle has **ovals** on each end.

Shapes on Cars

There are shapes on cars.

This car door looks like a **square**.

windshield

This windshield is shaped like a **rectangle**.

The **headlights** are **circles**.

Shapes on Fire Trucks

There are shapes on fire trucks.

Fire truck tires look like **circles**.

Look inside the fire truck.

There are circles, **squares,** and **rectangles!**

Shapes on Motorcycles

There are shapes on motorcycles.

The spokes on this wheel make many **triangles**.

The **headlight** on this motorcycle looks like a **circle**.

Shapes on Spacecraft

wings

There are shapes on spacecraft.

This **space shuttle** has wings shaped like **triangles**.

This **space station** has many long **rectangles**.

Shapes on Trains

There are shapes on trains.

Boxcars are shaped like **rectangles**.

This **tanker car** is a long **oval**.

The train wheels are **circles**.

Find the Shapes

Can you find squares?

Can you find circles?

Can you find triangles?

Can you find an oval?

Picture Glossary

blimp
page 7

headlight
pages 13, 17

rectangle
pages 5, 6, 9,
13, 15, 19, 20

square
pages 4, 12,
15

boxcar
page 20

kayak
page 11

seaplane
page 6

tanker car
page 21

circle
pages 4, 9, 13
14, 15, 17, 21

oval
pages 5, 7,
11, 21

**space
shuttle**
page 18

triangle
pages 4, 8, 10,
16, 18

frame
page 8

pedal
page 9

space station
page 19

Note to Parents and Teachers

Recognizing different geometric shapes is a key math concept. Help children learn how to classify basic shapes by pointing out the color outlines presented throughout the book and explaining their relationship with the image. Extend the activity on a walk around your school or neighborhood. Play a game of "I Spy," in which you tell the child that you spy a yellow triangle, red circle, and so on. See if the child can identify the object that you are thinking of. Then switch roles and have the child identify shapes while you guess what they are.

Index

Answers to quiz on page 22
These are the **squares, circles, triangles,** and **ovals.**